Coping with Life and Its Problems

Coping with Life and Its Problems

Joyce Marie Smith

TYNDALE HOUSE PUBLISHERS, INC.
Wheaton, Illinois

To my mother, Florence Braun,
for her love and encouragement.

Fifteenth printing, November 1984

Coping with Life and Its Problems
Library of Congress Catalog Card Number 76-47298
ISBN 0-8423-0437-7, paper
Copyright © 1976 by Tyndale House Publishers, Inc.
Wheaton, Illinois
Printed in the United States of America

Contents

Contents

Preface

This Bible study is written for Christ's believers who desire the ability to cope with all aspects and problems of life. In Christ we not only can cope, but experience triumph! Each lesson uses Bible examples of men and women who have also experienced many of the same problems or trials we face. This relevant and practical Bible study can be used individually or in groups.

"Now thanks be unto God, which always causeth us to triumph in Christ" (2 Corinthians 2:14, KJV).

Suggestions for the Leader

Self-Preparation

1. Be sure to prepare your own lesson thoroughly. Also try to read some of the recommended books.
2. Depend upon the Lord as you lead. Ask to be cleansed of sin, and filled with the Holy Spirit.

Guiding the Discussion

1. Pray for sensitivity to each woman's needs in your group. Pray for God's love for each one there.
2. Don't allow tangents to develop, discuss controversial issues, or get bogged down on any particular question.
3. Allow time at the end of the class for prayer. Pray topically or conversationally in short, honest prayers.
4. If the lesson seems long with a great deal of Scripture in it, you can either eliminate a few questions, have the women give their answers without reading the Scripture out loud in class, or just summarize the main thought of a group of Scriptures rather than discuss each separately.

Lesson One

Coping with Life's Pressures

You finally get the kids off to school ... you're having company tonight for dinner, so you rush to the grocery store to pick up some ingredients you need ... as room mother you have a list of names to call for your child's party at school ... your washing machine overflows, but the repair man can't come until tomorrow ... the school nurse calls and says your child is sick ... the phone rings incessantly ... and so it goes. Pressure and more pressure. A working woman experiences even more pressure, because of her added work load and less time for home and family.

Many of our pressures during the day are unavoidable, or beyond our control. But there are some which we can control.

Pressure and Priorities

There are some scriptural principles that can help us cope with life's pressures and tensions.

1. What are we told to do in Colossians 4:5 and Ephesians 5:16?

_____

To make the most of the twenty-four hours we each have, we must organize our time and establish our priorities.

2. Summarize your priorities and desires for the areas of your life listed below. Compare Proverbs 31:10-31.
   a. Your relationship to God _____
   _____
   _____
   b. Your relationship to your husband _____
   _____
   _____
   c. Your relationship to your children _____
   _____
   _____
   d. Your home and interests_____
   _____
   _____
   e. Your ministry in the community and church ____
   _____
   _____
   f. Your work outside the home (job) _____
   _____
   _____

3. Make a list each day this week of the things that need to be done according to your responsibilities and priorities. Cross them off as they are done. (This brings unbelievable satisfaction.)

4. The booklet *Tyranny of the Urgent* discusses the problem and danger of letting the urgent things each day crowd out the important. Our example in priorities with our time is Jesus Christ.
   a. What did Christ say concerning his work after three years? (John 17:4) _____
   b. What was Christ's secret? (Mark 1:35) _____
   _____
   c. From whom did Christ's direction come?_____

Promises for Pressure

5. What promises are given pertaining to life's pressures in these verses?

a. Matthew 11:28, 29 _____

_____

b. John 14:27 _____

_____

c. John 16:33 _____

_____

d. Ephesians 3:16 _____

_____

e. Philippians 4:6, 7 _____

_____

f. Philippians 4:13 _____

_____

g. Philippians 4:19_____

_____

h. James 1:2-4 _____

_____

6. The condition of our physical bodies has a lot to do with our ability to handle tension and pressures.

a. How much sleep do you need each day? _____
Do you get it? _____

b. What exercise program are you involved in?_____

_____

c. Do you need to change or improve eating habits?

_____

In *How to Handle Pressure,* Clyde and Ruth Narramore discuss specific ways to alleviate tension and pressure.

Fiery Furnace

There is another type of pressure which we as Christians might face regarding our beliefs.

7. Read Daniel 3:8-30.
   a. Why were Shadrach, Meshach, and Abed-nego punished? _____
   _____

   b. What was their witness under intense pressure (vv. 16-18)? _____
   _____

   c. How did God meet their needs (vv. 25-27)? _____
   _____

   d. What were the results (vv. 28-30)? _____
   _____

Summary

A little pressure can stimulate you in your work and help you accomplish more than you would otherwise. However, as pressure builds up through the day, it can have a draining and exhausting effect on you. As you learn to organize your time and evaluate your priorities, you will experience less pressure.

Application and Prayer

1. Did you evaluate your priorities? _____
2. In what areas do you still need more organization? (Learn to set deadlines!) _____
   _____
3. List some pressures you have today. What can you do about them?
   _____
   _____
   _____
4. Ask God to help you develop a calm and peaceful spirit to carry you through your pressures and tensions. Look to him for inner strength.

5. Ask God to help discipline your day to get the things done that he wants you to.

Recommended Reading

Hummel, Charles. *Tyranny of the Urgent*. Downers Grove, Ill.: InterVarsity, 1967.

King, Pat. *How Do You Find the Time*. Edmonds, Wash.: Aglow Publications, 1975.

Narramore, Clyde and Ruth. *How to Handle Pressure*. Wheaton, Ill.: Tyndale House, 1975.

Lesson Two

Coping with Disappointments and Hurts

Do you feel disappointed in your children's behavior or achievements? Have you been hurt by an unkind or insensitive word from your husband? Have friends disappointed you and let you down? Do you feel life has cheated you? Everyone experiences disappointments caused by circumstances, others, or failure to reach our own standards.

Let's look at some Bible characters and see how they coped with their disappointments.

A Multi-Colored Coat

1. Skim Genesis 37, 39, 40.
   List Joseph's disappointments and problems in life.

Disappointment	Reaction or Result for Good
a. Genesis 37:4, 5 _____	_____
b. Genesis 37:23-28_____	39:1-6_____
c. Genesis 39:17-20_____	39:21-23_____
d. Genesis 40:12-15, 23 ____	41:9-14_____

2. How do you think Joseph felt after each of these disappointments? _____

_____

3. Joseph experienced many disappointments and frustrations. But what testimony was he able to give in Genesis 45:5-8; 50:20? _____

_____

4. What were the ultimate benefits of Joseph's disappointments and problems? _____

List some disappointments you have experienced recently. What benefits could come from them? _____

_____

_____

He's Got the Whole World in His Hands

Joseph had a strong belief in the sovereignty of God. He knew God was ultimately in control of his life and his world regardless of how things looked on the surface.

5. Paraphrase Romans 8:28 in your own words. _____

_____

_____

6. Summarize these references on God's sovereignty over creation, mankind, or events.
   a. Romans 9:19-21 _____

_____

   b. Colossians 1:16, 17 _____

_____

   c. Psalm 24:1 _____

_____

7. How does God's sovereignty make you feel towards your disappointments and problems? _____

_____

I'm in Prison but Praising God

8. Read Acts 16:16-34.
   a. What was Paul's problem (vv. 19-24)?_____

   _____

   b. What was Paul's reaction (v. 25)?_____

   _____

   c. What were the results of his reaction (vv. 26-33)?

   _____

Particulars of Praise

Psalm 22:3 tells us that God inhabits our praises. He is among us when we praise him.

9. Summarize these commands about praising God.
   a. Psalm 33:1 _____

   _____

   b. Psalm 149:1 _____

   _____

   c. Philippians 4:4_____

   _____

   d. 1 Thessalonians 5:16-18_____

   _____

10. Share a result you have experienced by praising God.

   _____

   _____

11. What are some reasons given for problems and trials in life?
   a. Romans 5:3-5_____

   _____

   b. 2 Corinthians 1:3-5 _____

   _____

   c. James 1:1-5 _____

   _____

d. 1 Peter 1:6, 7 _____
_____

12. Share a problem you have experienced recently.
    Were you able to thank God for it?_____
    _____
    _____

Summary

Disappointments and problems are inevitable here on earth. It's the way we handle our disappointments that makes the difference.

Application and Prayer

1. Bring your disappointments and hurts to God in prayer. Claim 1 Peter 5:7.
2. Ask God to help you accept your situation.
3. Ask God for healing in your innermost being.
4. Begin to praise God for what he can do and teach you through your disappointments. Praise him that he is in control.
5. Praise God for himself and what he has done for you.

Recommended Reading

Carothers, Merlin. *Power in Praise*. Plainfield, N.J.: Logos, 1972.

Gossett, Don. *There's Dynamite in Praise*. Monroeville, Pa.: Whitaker House, 1974.

Rutledge, Howard and Phyllis. *In the Presence of Mine Enemies*. Old Tappan, N.J.: Revell, 1973.

Ten Boom, Corrie. *The Hiding Place*. Old Tappan, N.J.: Revell, 1971.

Lesson Three

Coping with Bitterness and Resentment

"He'll be sorry he did that to me." "I don't think I can ever forgive her for saying that." "It isn't fair that she got more than I did." Have you ever said anything like that?

A Bitter Spirit

1. Hannah's story in the Bible is familar to us. Let's see how she handled her bitterness. Read 1 Samuel 1:1-20.

   a. Why was Hannah unhappy (v. 5)? _____

   _____

   b. What made her condition unbearable (v. 6)? _____

   _____

   c. How did she react (vv. 7, 8, 10a)? _____

   _____

   d. Where did she find her answer (vv. 10b, 11)?

   _____

   e. What was the result regarding her bitterness (v. 18)? _____

   _____

   Instead of bitterness and resentment, what attitudes permeate her being (2:1-10)?_____

   _____

Deceit Reaps Bitterness

2. Describe Jacob and Esau's relationship (Genesis 25:27-34; 27:30-41).
   After being deceived by Jacob, Esau progressed in his feelings from _____ (Genesis 27:34, 38) to _____ (Genesis 27:41.). Because of the intensity of feelings, the two brothers were separated for over twenty years.

Seventy Times Seven

3. What commands are given regarding bitterness and unforgivingness?
   a. Matthew 5:21-25 _____

   b. Ephesians 4:31, 32 _____

   c. Colossians 3:19 _____

   d. Hebrews 12:15_____

4. What results from bitterness and unforgivingness in marriage and other relationships? _____

   None of These Diseases by S. I. McMillen discusses the physical results of bitterness and resentment.

5. Do you have a root of bitterness towards anyone today? God desires to cleanse you and deliver you from it. Steps for victory include: Confess it. Ask forgiveness and cleansing. Ask to be filled with the Holy Spirit. Ask the person wronged to forgive you. Do something to show your love.

6. What is a result of not forgiving others (Mark 11:25, 26)? Why?_____

_____
_____

7. Summarize these Scriptures:
   a. Matthew 18:21, 22 _____
   _____

   b. Luke 17:3, 4 _____
   _____

   c. Colossians 3:13 _____
   _____

8. Fill in the chart below:
                       Person   Example of Forgiveness
   a. Genesis 50:19-21 _____
   _____

   b. 1 Samuel 24:9-11 _____
   _____

   c. Luke 23:34 _____
   _____

   d. Acts 7:59, 60 _____
   _____

   e. 2 Timothy 4:16 _____
   _____

   Whom do you need to forgive today? _____

   Forgiveness involves action. Helen Kooiman's excellent book *Forgiveness in Action* describes the importance
of forgiveness as well as showing us how to forgive.

9. How are you to forgive? How has God forgiven you?
   Summarize these Scriptures.
   a. Psalm 103:12 _____
   _____

   b. Jeremiah 31:34 _____
   _____

   c. Isaiah 44:22 _____
   _____

d. Micah 7:19 _____

_____

e. 1 John 1:7, 9 _____

_____

Have you experienced God's forgiveness? _____

"Forgiveness restores the present, heals for the future, and releases us from the past," says David Augsburger.[1]

Summary

God's commands against resentment and bitterness are for our own protection and physical good. God is able to cleanse and deliver you from these sins. However, your will is involved in forgiving someone else. Are you willing to forgive?

Application and Prayer

1. Today ask forgiveness from anyone against whom you have resentment.
2. Forget the offense. Ask God to cleanse your mind of all grudges.

Recommended Reading

Augsburger, David. *Seventy Times Seven: The Freedom of Forgiveness*. Chicago, Ill.: Moody Press, 1970.

Kooiman, Helen. *Forgiveness in Action*. New York: Hawthorn Books, 1974.

McMillen, S. I. *None of These Diseases*. Old Tappan, N.J.: Revell, 1963.

[1]From *Seventy Times Seven: The Freedom of Forgiveness* by David Augsburger. Copyright 1970. Moody Press, Moody Bible Institute of Chicago. Used by permission.

Lesson Four

Coping with Broken Relationships

Friends who aren't speaking ... homes with an icy cold atmosphere ... children torn in their loyalties between an estranged mommy and daddy ... churches whose members are divided and at odds with each other ... teenagers who have left home in rebellion and anger—these are sad but unfortunately common examples of disrupted personal relationships.

Broken Relationships

Why do relationships break down and how can we repair these estrangements?

1. List some causes of broken relationships from the following Scriptures:
   a. Sarah and Hagar, Genesis 16:4-6 _____

   _____

   b. Jacob and Esau, Genesis 27:34-41 _____

   _____

   c. Rachel and Leah, Genesis 29:30-35; 30:1 _____

   _____

   d. Joseph and brothers, Genesis 37:3, 4, 8, 11 _____

   _____

   e. Saul and David, 1 Samuel 18:8-12, 16 _____

   _____

f. Paul and John Mark, Acts 15:37-40 _____

　　_____

Restored Relationships

2. List some reasons for reconciliation or explain why reconciliation did not occur.
　　a. Sarah and Hagar, Genesis 21:9-21 _____

　　_____

　　b. Jacob and Esau, Genesis 32:9-20; 33:4-11 _____

　　_____

　　c. Rachel and Leah, Genesis 30:1, 22-24 _____

　　_____

　　d. Joseph and his brothers, Genesis 45:4-8; 50:17-21

　　_____

　　_____

　　e. Saul and David, 1 Samuel 26:9-12_____

　　_____

　　f. Paul and John Mark, 2 Timothy 4:11 _____

　　_____

Father and Son

3. Let's study a broken relationship between a father and son (Luke 15:11-32).
　　a. Cause of the broken relationship (vv. 12, 13)____

　　_____

　　b. Consequences suffered by the son (vv. 14-16) ___

　　_____

　　c. Son's decision (vv. 17-20)_____

　　_____

　　d. Father's reaction (vv. 20-24) _____

　　_____

　　e. How the relationship was restored (v. 32) _____

　　_____

f. The elder brother's reaction (25-30) _____
_____

4. What did you learn about God the Father as symbolized in this Scripture? _____
_____

5. What are some other possible reactions the father might have had? _____
_____

What quality of spirit did the son have to have? ___
_____

What quality did the father demonstrate? _____
_____

6. Do you have a broken relationship with anyone today? _____

7. In Lesson 3 we discussed forgiveness, which also is an important aspect in restoring broken relationships. Do you have anyone else you should ask forgiveness from? _____

8. What aspects of communication need improvement in order to restore your broken relationships?
_____
_____
_____

9. Read 1 Corinthians 13:4-7, preferably in *The Living Bible*. List the aspects of love which you need to exhibit in your own life. _____
_____
_____

Summary

Broken relationships are a result of sin. As you are willing to confess your sin to God, healing can begin. God wants to bring healing to your broken relationships. He can develop his love in you for that other person. He can help you forgive and forget.

Application and Prayer

1. Obedience is important if you are to grow as a Christian. Have you initiated restoration of a broken relationship? _____

2. Develop the habit of immediate reconciliation in your friendships and relationships. Don't go to sleep at night until you are totally reconciled to your husband.

Recommended Reading

Goddard, Hazel B. *Can We Love Again?* Wheaton, Ill.: Tyndale House, 1971.

Jacobsen, Marion. *Crowded Pews and Lonely People.* Wheaton, Ill.: Tyndale House, 1972.

Lesson Five

Coping with Tragedy and Sorrow

How do you find consolation when you have just received a diagnosis that your four-year-old son has
leukemia? How do you adjust when your husband has
just lost his job? What solace do you find when faced
with the destruction of your home by fire? How do you
respond to the sudden accident which snuffs out the life
of your teenager?

Life does contain tragedies and sorrows. As Christians
we certainly are not exempt. In fact, God wants to show
his power through the witness of his people, a people
who are triumphant despite tragedy.

Boils and Blessings

1. Let's look at a man in the Bible who was faced with
   total destitution. Read Job 1; 2:1-8.
   a. Who did God allow to bring destruction to Job?

   _____

   b. List everything Job lost. _____

   _____

   c. How much did God allow? (2:6) _____

   _____

   d. What was Job's reaction? (2:10) _____

   _____

29

e. What was his wife's reaction? (2:9) _____

_____

f. What was the purpose of this testing? (1:9-12)___

_____

g. How was Job blessed later on? (42:12-17)_____

_____

How would you react in a situation like this? ___

_____

2. Have you ever experienced a "tragedy" that God used for good and you could later see a purpose for it? Share it with your discussion group.

God's Discipline

3. Read Hebrews 12:5-11 in several translations or paraphrases.
   a. Whom does the Lord discipline? (v. 6) _____

   _____

   b. What does discipline show? (vv. 7-9)_____

   _____

   c. Why does he discipline us? (vv. 6, 10) _____

   _____

   d. What are the results of his discipline? (v. 11) ___

   _____

4. List more results of God's discipline.
   a. John 15:2 _____
   b. 2 Corinthians 1:3, 4 _____
5. How have you recently experienced the discipline of God?_____

_____

6. What was your attitude? _____

_____

7. What was Paul's reaction to his "thorn in the flesh" (2 Corinthians 12:5-10)? _____

30

_____

What promise did God give him in 2 Corinthians 12:9?
_____

_____

_____

8. Share what God has taught you through some difficult experiences or tragedies. _____

_____

_____

Summary

God is not only a God of love, but he is also sovereign. As we come to accept his way of working in our lives, we will experience deep blessing and spiritual maturity.

Application and Prayer

1. When a tragedy or sorrow touches your life, learn to ask, "Lord, what do you want to teach me through this?"
2. Have you been practicing attitudes of acceptance and praise as discussed in Lesson 2?
3. Remember—God wants to help and strengthen you.

Recommended Reading

Carlson, C. C. *Straw Houses in the Wind*. Tustin, Calif.: Vision House Publishers, n.d.

Nee, Watchman. *The Release of the Spirit*. Sure Foundation Publications, 1965.

Lesson Six

Coping with Death and Pain

How do you react when someone you love is dying? Do you pretend it really isn't happening? Are you angry at God for allowing it? Do you bargain with God for that person's life? Does it cause you to go into depression? Or do you accept it? In her book *On Death and Dying,* Elisabeth Kubler-Ross enlarges on these five stages of reactions to death.

We don't know exactly what it is like to die; therefore, we can easily be afraid. But in Jesus Christ we can have peace and victory.

Reactions to Death

1. Describe the emotions these people experienced at the death of Lazarus in John 11.
   a. Martha (vv. 21, 22)_____
   b. Mary (vv. 31, 32) _____
   c. Jesus (vv. 35-38) _____
2. Joyce Landorf gives an honest description of her reaction to her mother's death in her book *Mourning Song.* Have you lost someone who was close to you? What emotions did you experience?

   _____

   _____

3. How did these people feel about death?
   a. Job, Job 19:25, 26 _____
   b. David, Psalm 23:4 _____
   c. Solomon, Ecclesiastes 3:1, 2 _____
   d. Christ, Matthew 26:39 _____
   e. Stephen, Acts 7:55-60 _____
   f. Paul, Philippians 1:21-23 _____
4. What two men were "translated" without experiencing death?
   a. Genesis 5:24; Hebrews 11:5 _____
   b. 2 Kings 2:11 _____

Our Hope

5. Hebrews 9:27 (KJV) says, "And as it is appointed unto men once to die, but after this the judgment." Death is an inevitable process. What is our hope in Jesus Christ?
   a. John 11:25, 26 _____
   b. John 14:1-3 _____
   c. John 14:19 _____
   d. 1 Corinthians 15:22 _____
   e. Hebrews 11:16 _____
   f. 1 Peter 1:3-9 _____
6. Read 1 Corinthians 15. This is a beautiful chapter setting forth the doctrine of Christ's resurrection and also his second coming. What effect does Christ's resurrection have on us (vv. 13-19)? _____

   _____

   _____

7. What makes us long for immortality?
   a. 1 Corinthians 15:53-57 _____

   _____

b. 2 Corinthians 5:1-4 _____

_____

c. Philippians 1:23 _____

_____

8. Which Scriptures were most comforting to you in this lesson? _____

_____

Summary

Sometimes we are not so afraid of death itself as the process of death or the pain involved with some dread disease. As we trust God with our life, we can also trust him with our death and pain. He will be with us and meet each need we have. Death is a process whereby we are liberated from our bodies and so experience the delights and pleasures of being with our Lord and Savior Jesus Christ.

Application and Prayer

1. Have you and your husband or loved ones made your wills and prepared for your deaths? _____

2. Have you prepared your children for death? How?

_____

3. Are you preparing yourself spiritually for death? Are you ready? _____

Recommended Books

Kubler-Ross, Elisabeth. *On Death and Dying*. New York: MacMillan, 1970.

Landorf, Joyce. *Mourning Song*. Old Tappan, N.J.: Revell, 1974.

Smith, Joyce. *The Significance of Jesus*. Wheaton, Ill.: Tyndale House, 1976.

Lesson Seven

Coping with
Loneliness

A president of a huge corporation ... a single girl ... an elderly widower ... a homemaker—what characteristic can all these have in common? Loneliness. Loneliness is no respecter of persons, plaguing the rich as well as the poor, the young as well as the old. You don't even have to be alone to be lonely—you can be in the middle of a crowd and still be lonely! Loneliness has been a universal problem for all mankind.

It's Lonely at the Top

1. Let's look at some scriptural examples of loneliness:

	Man	*Situation*
a. Genesis 6:5-18		
b. Exodus 18:13-18		
c. Matthew 26:36-46		
d. 2 Timothy 4:9-11		

2. Share an experience when you have been lonely. ___

37

3. In what two areas does God provide for this need?
   a. 1 Corinthians 12:12-27; Hebrews 10:25 _____
   _____

   b. Matthew 28:20b; Hebrews 13:5b_____
   _____

On Being Alone

4. How can we better meet the needs of lonely people in our churches? List a specific action which could be taken for the following people to help in their times of loneliness.
   a. a widow _____
   b. a divorcee_____
   c. a college student away from home _____
   _____

   d. a single career person _____
   e. an invalid _____
   f. a new person in town _____
   g. a friend adjusting to a recent bereavement_____
   _____

   h. a high schooler with non-Christian parents_____
   _____

   i. a woman with a non-Christian husband who doesn't attend church _____
   _____

   j. parents of a severely handicapped child _____
   _____

5. Do any (or all) of these people attend your church? Covenant with God to minister to at least two of these types of individuals soon. Reach out to them in loving concern.
6. Let's look at our Scripture examples again and see how they coped with their loneliness.

a. Noah, Genesis 6:22 _____

_____

b. Moses, Exodus 18:17-26 _____

_____

c. Christ, Matthew 26:39 _____

_____

d. Paul, 2 Timothy 4:17, 18 _____

_____

Love Yourself

7. One of the biggest causes of loneliness is a low self-esteem. Elizabeth Skoglund writes, ''Good self-esteem exists where intellectually as well as emotionally one makes an honest evaluation of himself. Then what he doesn't like he improves upon until he can genuinely like and accept himself... Along with self-esteem, relationships with other people are a second vital factor in the problem of loneliness ... Good self-esteem helps in forming good relationships which in turn build good self-esteem.''[1]

8. Summarize these verses relating to acceptance of ourselves:

a. Exodus 4:10, 11 _____

_____

b. Isaiah 45:9 _____

_____

c. Jeremiah 18:1-4 _____

_____

9. In Philippians 1:6 and Ephesians 2:10, what promises

---

[1]From *Loneliness* by Elizabeth Skoglund. © 1975 by Inter-Varsity Christian Fellowship of the USA. Used by permission from InterVarsity Press.

are given regarding God's work in our lives? _____
_____

10. One way of creating a better self-esteem is to develop and use the spiritual gifts and talents God has given you. List the spiritual gifts you are now using. _____
_____

11. Your relationship to God is of utmost importance in enjoying inner security and confidence, and in alleviating loneliness. What are you doing to develop your Christian growth?_____
_____
_____

12. Summarize:
    a. Colossians 2:6, 7_____
    _____

    b. Ephesians 5:18 _____
    _____

    c. 1 Peter 2:2, 3 _____
    _____

    d. 1 Thessalonians 5:16-18_____
    _____

Summary

All of us experience loneliness from time to time. The antidote is to be concerned about others and their needs. Depend on Jesus to meet your needs—he wants to be your friend.

Application and Prayer

1. Become more sensitive to the needs of lonely people around you. Reach out to help others!
2. Ask God to help you accept and love yourself.

Recommended Reading

Skoglund, Elizabeth. *Loneliness*. Downers Grove, Ill.: InterVarsity Press, 1975.

Lesson Eight

Coping with Materialism

You never seem to have enough money, even with your husband's occasional salary increases. Not only did the cost of groceries go up during the year, but clothes expenses for the family seemed to double! Your friends have nicer clothes than you do and they seem to eat out a lot too. You'd like to travel more, and maybe paint the house.

As Christians, how do we keep our finances in the proper perspective and cope with materialistic pressure?

Pillar of Salt

1. What are some examples of materialism in the Scriptures?

                                    Person   Act/Result
   a. Genesis 13:5-13 _____
   b. Genesis 19:23-26 _____
   c. Matthew 19:16-22 _____
   d. Matthew 26:14-16 _____
   e. Luke 12:16-21 _____
      Do you know of similar examples today? _____
      _____

2. What are some positive examples toward worldly possessions and riches?

Person   *Act/Result*

a. Matthew 4:19-22; _____

Luke 18:28 _____

b. Mark 12:41-43 _____

c. Philippians 4:11, 12 _____

3. Are these examples relevant for today? Why or why not?

_____

Outside Influences

4. What do you believe is the influence of television on these areas:
a. values and priorities_____

b. desire for goods _____

c. discontent_____

d. home life_____

e. use of time _____

What other influences from the world affect us? ___

5. What are Christians called in Hebrews 11:13-16?___

What effect should this have on our values?_____

Dig Up the Root

6. What is a root of various evils (1 Timothy 6:10)? Compare Luke 16:14. Why is this? _____ _____

_____

7. Summarize these commands regarding values and possessions:

   a. Matthew 6:19-21 _____

   _____

   b. Matthew 6:25-34 _____

   _____

   c. Hebrews 13:5 (compare 1 Timothy 6:8)_____

   _____

   d. 1 John 2:15, 16 _____

   _____

   What has God convicted you of through these verses? _____

   _____

The Choice

8. Ultimately our attitudes depend on whom we serve. Read Matthew 6:24. Why is it necessary to make a choice?_____

   _____

   _____

9. Summarize these Scriptures regarding giving to the Lord's work.

	Command or Example	*Promise, If Any*
a. Genesis 28:22		
b. Malachi 3:8-11		
c. Luke 6:38		
d. Romans 12:8		
e. 2 Corinthians 9:7		

45

What blessings have you experienced through giving? _____

_____

God, Money and You is an excellent book on attitudes and scriptural principles regarding finances.

10. God promises to meet your needs and delights in prospering you. What conditions for prosperity are given here:
    a. Genesis 39:23 _____
    b. Deuteronomy 29:9 _____
    c. Joshua 1:8 _____
    d. Psalm 1:2, 3 _____

Summary

Matthew 6:21 (KJV) says, "For where your treasure is, there will your heart be also." Where is your treasure?

Application and Prayer

1. Are your material possessions in their proper perspective? _____
2. Are you keeping a monthly budget and record of expenditures? _____
3. Are you and your family giving at least ten percent of your income? Discuss this lesson with your husband.
4. Ask God to take away covetousness for "things." Ask him to help you discipline your spending.
5. One of the Hebrew names for God, Jehovah-Jireh, means "the Lord our Provider." Claim his provision for your needs financially.

Recommended Reading

Otis, George. *God, Money and You*. Old Tappan, N.J.: Revell, 1972.

Coping with Lusts and Temptations

The minister runs off with the church organist ... a deacon is cited for income tax evasion ... an elder's daughter has to get married ... the president of the woman's group is forty-five pounds overweight ... a Sunday school teacher resigns because his new speedboat lures him away on weekends. Yes, these are all Christians, and they have one thing in common—they have given in to temptation.

Reactions to Temptation

1. Let's look at some Bible examples of temptation.

	Reaction to	
Person	*Temptation*	*Result*
a. Genesis 3 _____		
_____		
b. 2 Samuel 11:1-17 _____		
_____		
c. Mark 14:66-71 _____		
_____		
d. Acts 5:1-10 _____		
_____		

2. Draw a line matching the person with the type of sin he yielded to:

Peter	Lying to the Holy Spirit
David	regarding money
Eve	Denying Christ
Ananias and Sapphira	Independence, disobedience
	Immorality

3. In contrast, note the reaction of the following people to temptation:

Person	Temptation	Reaction

a. Genesis 39:7-12 _____

_____

b. 2 Corinthians 12:7-9 _____

_____

c. Hebrews 4:15_____

_____

4. Using a Bible concordance, find Scriptures which give commands and insights on the following temptations and lusts:
   a. Immorality _____
   b. Overeating _____
   c. Covetousness_____
   d. Selfish behavior _____
   e. Can you think of any others (and Scriptures that talk about them)? _____

   _____

   Has God convicted you in any of these areas? Which ones? _____

   _____

Like a Roaring Lion

5. In James 1:13, 14 we are reminded that God himself does not tempt us to sin. Who does tempt us (Luke 4:1, 2; 1 Thessalonians 3:5)?_____

What temptation have you experienced recently? __

_____

6. How are we told to react to temptation and Satan's attacks?
   a. Matthew 26:41 _____

   _____

   b. Galatians 6:1 _____

   _____

   c. Ephesians 6:16 _____

   _____

   d. 1 Peter 5:8, 9 _____

   _____

Greater Is He

7. What promises does God give us?
   a. 1 Corinthians 10:13_____

   _____

   b. 2 Peter 2:9 _____

   _____

   c. 1 John 4:4_____

   _____

8. Why do we know Christ can help us? (Compare Matthew 4, Luke 4.)
   a. Hebrews 2:18_____
   b. Hebrews 4:15_____
   Thank Jesus that he is interceding for you right now.
9. What blessings result from temptation?
   a. James 1:2-4 _____

   _____

   b. James 1:12 _____

   _____

Share a blessing you have experienced from a temptation or test of your faith. _____

10. What example does Jesus give us in his prayers?
    a. Matthew 26:36-44 _____

    _____

    b. John 17:15 _____

    _____

    Are you facing a temptation right now? Ask your
    group to pray for you.
11. Meditate on Ephesians 6:10-18. Saturate your mind
    with God's offensive method of attack against Satan.

Summary

Everyone is tempted. It is our reaction to the temptation that makes the difference. Through testing, our faith
grows and becomes strong. Jesus wants to help us in our
temptations. Romans 8:37 (KJV) says, "In all these
things we are more than conquerors through him that
loved us."

Application and Prayer

1. Pray for your husband, children, and friends today,
   that God would protect them and help them in their
   temptations.
2. Be alert and prepared for Satan's attacks.
3. Be prepared spiritually through prayer and studying
   the Word.
4. Thank Jesus for the inner strength he wants to give
   you.

Recommended Reading

Harrah, Allegra. *Prayer Weapons*. Old Tappan, N. J.:
Revell, 1976.

Stedman, Ray. *Spiritual Warfare*. Waco, Tex.: Word,
n.d.

Coping with Lack of Purpose

Do you feel bored each day, with no real reason to even get out of bed? Do you lack a sense of direction and purpose in living? Or do you wonder how to get out of the rat race of life? Lack of purpose can cause depression, unhappiness, and unproductivity.

Finding Purpose

1. List God's general purposes for you.
   a. Romans 8:29 _____
   b. Isaiah 43:7; Revelation 4:11 _____
   _____
   c. John 15:8; Ephesians 2:10_____
   _____
   d. Ephesians 4:13 _____
   _____

   Your basic purpose in creation is "to enjoy God and glorify him forever." Do you feel you are fulfilling this purpose? _____
2. What purposes for women are given here?
   a. Genesis 1:28_____
   b. Genesis 2:18_____
   c. 1 Corinthians 11:9_____

51

How are you fulfilling these purposes? How can you improve? _____

_____

3. What was Christ's purpose on earth?
   a. Matthew 20:28; Mark 10:45 _____

   _____

   b. John 13:14-16_____

   _____

   c. 1 Timothy 2:6 _____

   _____

4. What type of life does Christ offer us?
   a. John 4:14 _____

   _____

   b. John 10:10b _____

   _____

5. As we reach out and minister to others' needs, we actually find our own needs being met! Sharing Christ with others adds lasting joy and meaningful purpose to our lives. Who have you ministered to recently? _____

List several people you know who have needs or are experiencing hurts. Pray for them. Try to do something to show your concern and love. _____

_____

Decisions, Decisions

6. Another factor in having a sense of purpose is that of understanding God's will. Several signs pointing to God's will are—the Bible, prayer, inner peace, and counsel with Christian friends. List the specific will of God already revealed to us.
   a. Ephesians 5:17, 18 _____

   _____

b. 1 Thessalonians 4:3 _____

_____

c. 1 Thessalonians 5:18 _____

_____

d. 1 Timothy 2:1-4 _____

_____

e. 1 Peter 2:13-15 _____

_____

In what areas do you want to know God's will?

_____

7. Summarize these promises regarding guidance.

Promise   Condition, If Any

a. Psalm 25:9 _____

_____

b. Psalm 32:8 _____

_____

c. Proverbs 3:5, 6 _____

_____

d. John 10:3, 4, 27 _____

_____

Claim a promise for a particular need you have. Thank God for these promises, and by faith expect to receive his guidance and direction.

8. Let's look at some Bible examples of guidance.

Person   God's Direction

a. 1 Samuel 3:1-14 _____

_____

b. Acts 9:3-7 _____

_____

c. Acts 16:6, 7 _____

_____

d. Acts 16:9, 10 _____

_____

e. Luke 4:1 _____

   _____

      Share an experience you have had of God's direc-
      tion and guidance.

      _____

      _____
      _____

 9. What promise is given in James 1:5, 6? _____

    _____

10. Sometimes we want to know God's will all at once.
    What did Jesus tell the apostles in Acts 1:6, 7? ____

    _____

Summary

   It is important that we as Christians know our purpose
in life and have a willingness to obey God's will as he
reveals it to us. Jesus wants to give us an abundant and
fulfilling life!

Application and Prayer

 1. In what areas do you feel greater purpose after study-
    ing this lesson?

    _____

    _____

 2. Did you thank him for his promises in Question 7?

    _____

 3. Ask God to help you obey him.

Recommended Reading

   Fromer, Paul *et al*. *Essays on Guidance (His Reader,*
Vol. 3). Downers Grove, Ill.: InterVarsity Press, 1968.
   MacArthur, John. *God's Will Is Not Lost*. Wheaton,
Ill.: Victor Books, 1973.

Lesson Eleven

Coping with Hopelessness

Sleeping pills, a gun, a noose, exhaust fumes in a car, drugs—one person every minute uses one of these tools to destroy himself. Suicide is too frequently a dead-end answer to life's problems and pressures. A suicide victim can find no reason for hope. As we study the cause of suicide, we will also discover God's basis for victorious living.

"I Want to Die"

1. Moses was a leader of two million people and was overwhelmed with the frustrations of his responsibilities. Read Numbers 11:10-18.

   a. The cause of his hopelessness (vv. 4-6, 10) _____

   _____

   b. His reaction (vv. 14, 15) _____

   _____

   c. God's solution (vv. 16-18)_____

   _____

2. Elijah, exhausted after his victory over Baal, was unable to cope with threats. Read 1 Kings 19:1-8.

   a. The cause of his despair (vv. 1, 2) _____

   _____

   b. His reaction (v. 4) _____

   _____

c. God's solution (vv. 5-8)_____

_____

3. To Jonah's amazement, wicked Nineveh experienced revival. Read Jonah 4:1-11 to see his reaction to this.
   a. The cause of his depression (vv. 1, 2) _____

   _____

   b. His reaction (vv. 3, 8) _____

   _____

   c. God's solution (vv. 6-11)_____

4. What different emotions did these three men experience? _____

   _____

   The end result in them was depression and hopelessness.
5. Read Acts 16:23-34. What triggered the jailer's action in verse 27?_____

   _____

   What did he do in verses 30-34? _____

   _____

   The beginning of victory is accepting Christ as Savior, and then walking in him.
6. Who committed suicide in Matthew 27:3-5 and why?

   _____

   Going Sideways is an excellent book which discusses the causes of and answers to suicide.

7. Discuss together causes of depression and hopelessness in these areas:
   a. Physical _____

   _____

   b. Mental_____

   _____

c. Emotional_____

_____

d. Spiritual _____   _____

_____

Discouragement, Despondency, Despair

Tim LaHaye's book *How to Win Over Depression* provides a helpful study on the problem of depression, and on experiencing victory in Christ.

8. How did these men handle their feelings of despondency?

| | *Man* | *His Reactions* |

a. Job 13:15 _____

_____

b. Psalm 40:1-4; 42; 43:5 _____

_____

c. 2 Corinthians 12:9; Philippians 4:13 _____

_____

9. The key area which needs to be controlled to prevent depression, despair, and hopelessness is our mind. Our mind is a battleground. What do these verses say about our thoughts?

a. Proverbs 4:23_____

_____

b. Proverbs 23:7_____

_____

c. Matthew 12:34, 35 _____

_____

10. Who knows and understands our thoughts (Psalm 139:2)? _____

Who is our example and pattern (Philippians 2:5)?

_____

11. With what are we to fill our mind (Philippians 4:7-9)?

_____

_____

12. Summarize the commands regarding our minds found in Ephesians 4:23; Romans 12:2; 2 Timothy 1:7 (KJV). _____

_____

13. Satan is the usurper of our souls. He is the one who wants to destroy us. What role do our thoughts play in this? See 2 Corinthians 10:3-5.

_____

_____

Summary

We do not need to wallow in hopelessness and despair. Our hope is Jesus Christ. He is the answer to the causes of depression and despair. He alone brings victory over Satan's attacks. He can help us control our thoughts and can give us hope for living.

Application and Prayer

1. Do you have a problem with negative thinking? Discouragement? Despair? God can help you control your thoughts as well as your feelings.
2. Trust Christ to work in your mind and in your family, praying for protection from Satan's attacks.

Recommended Reading

Haggai, John E. *How to Win Over Worry*. Grand Rapids, Mich.: Zondervan, 1959.

LaHaye, Tim. *How to Win Over Depression*. Grand Rapids, Mich.: Zondervan, 1974.

Pederson, Duane; Kooiman, Helen. *Going Sideways*. New York: Hawthorn Books, 1974.

Sanders, J. Oswald. *A Spiritual Clinic*. Chicago, Ill.: Moody Press, 1958.

Smith, Joyce Marie. *Learning to Talk with God*. Wheaton, Ill.: Tyndale House, 1976.

The Ultimate Answer to Coping with Life

We have been studying how to cope with different types of problems, pressures, and traumas in life. Our premise has been that you have believed in and accepted Jesus Christ as your own personal Savior. (See John 1:12; 3:16, 36; 1 John 5:11-13; Revelation 3:20.)

God's desire for us is that we experience abundant, fruitful, and victorious lives for him. This lesson deals with how to experience this abundant life.

Two Ways of Life

1. Describe the two contrasting ways of life for the Christian.

   Carnal Christian

   a. Romans 7:15-25 _____

   _____

   1 Corinthians 3:1-3 _____

   _____

   Spirit-Filled Christian

   b. Galatians 5:16, 18, 22, 23 _____

   _____

   Romans 8:1, 2, 6 _____

   _____

Romans 12:1, 2 _____

_____

Colossians 3:12-14 _____

_____

Which type of life brings peace and joy? _____
Which type of life honors God and brings eternal
fruit? _____

A Dead Man

3. Colossians 3:3 says we are _____. (Compare
   Galatians 2:20.)
4. How can this crucifixion of self (flesh) be experienced?

   _____

   _____

Read Romans 6 in several translations for clarification
and understanding. Summarize on a separate sheet the
key truths taught in verses 6, 11, 13, 16. The results of
death to self are seen in Romans 8, as the Spirit-filled life
is described.

Appropriating Christ's Life

5. How can we be filled with the Holy Spirit and experience the abundant life Jesus wants us to have? All
   Christians are indwelt by the Holy Spirit, but not all
   are filled and controlled by him.
   a. What command is given in Ephesians 5:18?_____

      _____

   b. How is the Holy Spirit received (Galatians 3:14b)?

      _____

   c. What are we told to do in Luke 11:13? _____

      _____

Stop right now and ask to be filled with the Holy Spirit. Then thank him that he answered your prayer. Each morning yield yourself to him and ask to be filled anew.

6. As we daily depend upon his fullness in our lives, we will truly experience 2 Corinthians 2:14 (KJV)— "Now thanks be unto God, which always causeth us to triumph in Christ."

   Summarize the results of the Spirit-filled life.

   a. Galatians 5:22, 23 _____

   _____

   b. Acts 1:8 _____

   _____

   c. John 7:37-39_____

   _____

7. Read Paul's prayer in Ephesians 3:16-21, preferably from *The Living Bible*. Claim this prayer for yourself, your husband, children, or friends.

8. How can we cope with life's pressures; disappointments and hurts; bitterness and resentment; broken relationships; tragedy and sorrow; death and pain; loneliness; materialism; lusts and temptations; lack of purpose; hopelessness? Jesus Christ is our only answer. He longs to help us with each problem or hurt we experience.

9. Read Colossians 2:6, 7 in *The Living Bible*.

   Write a paragraph summarizing what you have learned from Lesson 12 about experiencing daily victory in your life.

   _____

   _____

   _____

   _____

   _____

Summary

The Christian life should be an exciting, victorious adventure. Even as we made the initial choice to accept him as Savior, we can choose the Spirit-filled walk.

Application and Prayer

1. Did your response to Question 4 include asking for forgiveness and cleansing?
2. Did you ask to be filled with the Holy Spirit in Question 5?
3. Trust Christ with your daily problems even as you trusted him for salvation.
4. Thank God that he is indwelling you, empowering you, sanctifying you. Claim the victory God has already given you.

Recommended Reading

Meyer, F. B. *The Christ-Life for Your Life*. Chicago, Ill.: Moody Press, n.d.

Paxson, Ruth. *Rivers of Living Water*. Chicago, Ill.: Moody Press, n.d.

Thomas, W. I. *The Saving Life of Christ*. Grand Rapids, Mich.: Zondervan, 1961.